Chime

Poems

Len Lawson

Copyright © 2019 by Len Lawson

All rights reserved. No part of this book may be reproduced in any manner without written consent except for the quotation of short passages used inside of an article, criticism, or review.

Get Fresh Books, LLC
PO BOX 901
Union, New Jersey 07083

getfreshbooksllc.com

ISBN: 978-0-9989358-6-7
Control Number: email info@getfreshbooksllc.com

Cover image: "They Want Us, But With Our Black Off" by Cedric Umoja

Cover design & book layout: Ann Davenport

Contents

America.	1
black body be like	2
Groundhog Day	3
Self-Portrait as a Slave Ship	8
Battle Royal (Two Brown Boys)	10
the body is a cave	13
Hymn to the Tiki God	15
Power Outage in South Carolina	16
For the Dead Whose Caskets Flowed Out of Graves	17
Love Letter for South Carolina	19
A Blind Man Gives You [In] Sight	21
Plan B	22
Racism Is as American as _____	24
When a White Man in Camden Tells You to Act Like You Got Some Sense	27
Niger (or the Country with a Missing Letter)	29
You've Heard This Before	33
Snap Beans	34
The Black Body Is a Wind Chime	36
I'm Human Too	37
We're Talking about Practice	39
His Majesty	41
I Pass Liberty Seafood Every Day	42
The Body Is a Door	44
Skinny Boy	46

Down South	48
I Was Born with No Middle Name	50
The Body Is a God	51
The Nightclub // Is a Funeral // Is a Nightclub	52
How Not to Dissect a Frog	54
In Which People Say *You Look Like Buuud from The Cosby Show*	55
Going to Court in My Hometown	59
The Body Is a Rustic Bag	60
Not Stopping at a Police Checkpoint at 5 AM after Buffing Floors All Night and Feeling High from the Fumes	61
Acknowledgments	63
Thank You(s)	64
About the Author	66

Some days the chimes raged.
Some days they hung still.

"The Wind Chimes" by Shirley Buettner

Chime

America.

A dark-skinned mother of triplets weeps
holding her infants for the first time.

With sweat pooling in her gullet
she announces to the hospital room

*These children will be called
Ferguson, Baltimore, and Charleston.*

The babies cycle around the room
through several nurses' hands.

One of them conveys the news
of their names to the father in

the waiting area. He glances
at the rapid fire sun rioting

through the window.
Sweat angers a necklace

around his button shirt.
A terror slaps his eyes

back at the nurse like daggers.
He slices her joy with a whisper.

*Babies are being born
to weeping black mothers*

*all over this country
right now!*

*Tell me their names!
Tell me they matter!*

black body be like

```
            forgotten     foreskin
                          like
sweet steps through a     chocha       jungle
                          like
                          vibrator     razor to the epidermis
                          like
            train of      chinchilla   in December
                          like
Mama's whirlwind          breath       after her baby boy's funeral
                          like
*Don't put me to bed   No sleep*
                          like
                          eyes    memorizing the other side of the universe
                          like
            *Don't*        wake me    I'm sleep*
                          like
     *Breathe Mama*        breathe
                          like
            butterfly     kiss   from mink
                          like
                 silky    skin          of a hatchet
                          like
goose bumps on            areolas
                          like
king & queen in darkest Africa
                          like
armor    of black         savage
```

Groundhog Day

Wake up
Shower
Brush teeth and hair
Lotion with cocoa butter
Get dressed
Drink coffee
Drive to work
Drive home
Stopped by police
Demanded to show license
Ask why
Get cursed out
Curse back
Reach for license
Dead

Wake up
Shower
Brush teeth and hair
Lotion with cocoa butter
Get dressed
Drink coffee
Drive to work
Drive home
Stopped by police
Demanded to show license
Be polite
Explain you have a family
Be polite
Explain you are reaching for license
Dead

Wake up
Shower

Brush teeth and hair
Lotion with cocoa butter
Get dressed
Drink coffee
Drive to work
Drive home
Stopped by police
Demanded to show license
Be polite
Ask how cop's day is going
Get angry at response about too many niggers on the streets
Attempt reasonable conversation on diversity
Get cursed out
Screamed at to show license
Do nothing
Get jerked by the collar
Stay frozen
Gun aimed in your face
Stay frozen
Not even blinking
Get dragged out of car
Attempt to stand
Dead

Wake up
Shower
Brush teeth and hair
Lotion with cocoa butter
Get dressed
Drink coffee
Drive to work
Drive home
Stopped by police
Demanded to show license
Drive
Drive

Drive
Get chased by cop
then another, then another, then another
until you lead a troop of squad cars through town
Poke head out of window
Laugh maniacally
Smile at chopper overhead
Drive onto the interstate
Get cheered by other black men standing by
Remember your family
See your wife's face crying at her TV
See your child asking Mommy tough questions about Daddy
See your phone ring in the car
Answer with *Baby, I love you*
Get asked, *Why are you doing this*
Answer, *It's the only way out*
Hear screams of *Come home*
Hear child yell, *Come home, Daddy*
Hear chopper blades and sirens with wife's yelling
Stop the car
Get out
Raise hands over your head
Say to police, *I want to go home*
Dead

Wake up
Shower
Brush teeth and hair
Lotion with cocoa butter
Get dressed
Drink coffee
Drive to nearest pawnshop
Buy gun
Drive to work
Leave gun in car
Drive home

Stopped by police
Demanded to show license
Grab gun under seat
Point at approaching cop
Relish in cop's fear before screaming, *Is this what you want?!*
Point gun at self
Dead

Wake up
Shower
Brush teeth and hair
Lotion with cocoa butter
Get dressed
Drink coffee
Drive to work
Look up cop online
Research his credentials
Search for his family on social media
Find his wife
Find their address
Leave work
Go to cop's home
Greet cop's wife at the door
Explain that her husband has killed you each of the last five days
Ask why her husband hates black people
Ask how you can convince her husband
that you are a man with a family who wants a bright future for his child
See three police cars pull up behind you
See her husband get out
Realize she called the police before you approached the door
Raise hands and kneel to the ground
Close your eyes and whisper to your wife you love her
Get beat down by police on the pavement
Get thrown into cop car
Feel broken bones and see with blurry vision out of only one eye
Ask cop how many black men he has killed

Hear him cackle and say, *Not enough*
All of them if I could
Do not survive car ride to jail
Dead

Wake up
Kiss your wife
Kiss your child
Brush teeth and hair
Observe the wisdom and grace of the scarf on your wife's head
Lotion with cocoa butter
Remember the smell of your child moments after leaving the womb
Get dressed
Hug your wife
Hug your child
Cry at the sight of your child's bright face
Pick up child in your arms
Notice the eyes, nose, and smile like yours
Tell your family you won't be home tonight
Hear your shocked wife ask why
Answer through tears, *I don't know*
Maybe one day
But maybe not today

Self-Portrait as a Slave Ship

Chromosomes chained side by side
can only piss on each other for comfort
I am one titanic mitochondrion
My belly vomits out ocean waves

My language doesn't match the captain's
He can't understand my body's sounds
My groans must be taught in Victorian-style
buildings pointing to the ocean that is

heaven where I sit at the
bottom of praying to drown
His people must walk single file balancing
mortar boards on the safes atop

their necks where they hope the conjugations
and tenses do not escape after graduation
I am shackled through strange eyes and I
weep for the homeland birth canal

    Mama's dark belly
    Wonderful people live there
    I miss them all now

My screams below deck are
a threat to the conscience of this hour
The rumble of my tribe within Her erupts
with every drum beat in my chest

Turn this vessel around and
take me back where I belong
No one can navigate me
I am the captain now

    Ain't no going back

Not even if the bodies
black within revolt

Battle Royal (Two Brown Boys)

Two brown boys in a Carolina wood
    white boys meander both
                      manifest destiny

    White boy says   *Y'all two should fight*
        cock fight
        dog fight
                White boy knows both already lost

Two brown boys square off
    one from Africa   white boys don't know what tribe
    one from Bangladesh   all they see is a Muslim

Two brown boys dance and pivot each other
            Alvin Ailey is proud
    one with scraped knees bordered by peeled scabs
        the legacy of whips and shackles
    one with sweaty brow mopped by sprouts of hair
      down to the collar of a black flannel top
      tucked into acid-washed jeans
            American history

Two brown boys blistered by white eyes
        on the sidelines
      waiting for blood
        placing bets
passing the time until the recess bell signals
    the race to classes
        celebrating
        a blank-page history

    They are all the eye of a cyclops
        white sclera
        trembling brown iris

                    black pupil taking in light and darkness

Two brown boys stare at each other
then around the white boy ring
then back at each other
Muslim kid advances with a flurry of punches
        Black kid blocks
balances the equation

 Two brown boys sucking wind
            gulps of blood they swallow
        slow-dripped from the American flag
        above them in the schoolyard

African boy goes in for the kill
        without spear or dagger
tackles Muslim kid to the grass
applies headlock

Good enough? he laughs nervously

            Cyclops shuts its eye in slumber
Black boy pumps fists into the ominous gray sky
        shouts of tribal euphoria
glares around the white boy ring for approval
            soul open to receive the prize for
            second class on the schoolyard

 No one hoists him on their shoulders

He happy 'cause he beat a Muslim, they say
and hold their aching bellies full of laughs
birthed from guilty pangs a generation ahead

            Bell sounds
White boy ring dissolves

Two brown boys left
staring into the broken mirror of each other's face

            Cyclops won't appreciate
                its monstrous eye
          for another generation ahead

    Ol' Glory tumbles above to usher in
the storm from some foreign land
      licks the storm with its own stripes

brown grass recovers
      braces for the storm with a sigh

the body is a cave

bullet hole in the globe

      implode a mountain and echo into the wound

wet embrace for a warm shank

      open tomb where a messiah once lay
got up and left his deathbed unmade

          this body is uncomfortable for a Christ

      whistle into it and melody
cries out bats

      as a child, i always covered my eyes in school
from the voluptuous body of the word *spelunking*

      a mouth with toothless rancor
the body is a gum hole
                deeply rooted bone once grew here

      the body is an eye slammed shut
plucked out because it offends so many

            still whistles back its
                rogue nocturnal creatures

      the body is a howling from
the unknown in the wilderness

          praying to know from what animal it comes

      the cave is a body
dark cold dead body

       man's finest still bring their best instruments
  to burst it open and sew it shut

      to fear it
to fear losing it
             inside them

Hymn to the Tiki God
for Charlottesville

You revisited them at a Pentecost not prophesied
    In a small college town in Virginia where hundreds of

The sons of your former believers gathered not in your name
    But in the names of themselves above every other name

They blazed your bamboo torches to rekindle what was left
    Of the light you brought to the masses from a hemisphere away

Without painted faces and tribal masks
    They waged war on the idolatry in equality for all men

They hoisted your symbol of peace and tranquility to
    Invoke hate and sameness in the face of the god of the Other

And you from the golden calf throne their fathers created now ask
    Where are your Hawaiian shirts and your fruity mixed drinks

And your hula skirts and your tribal dances
    Where are my sirens who entranced you to my islands

By their Tiki torch serpents they waved your incense of fire
    Ignominiously in the face of a god who bears the same

Could their white privilege not have procured
    The Olympic torch itself or could they not have

Implored Prometheus a second time to risk his eternity
    We implore you to quench their hate and spew its ashes across the sea

Let the smoke rise to your throne for a sweet fragrance
    Where you can rest in perpetual peace from being summoned again

Power Outage in South Carolina
  after Hurricanes Matthew, Florence, & Michael

Half the state lives in darkness
The left greets the sun
relegating the right to await
Mother Earth unveiling her
countenance after a hurricane has
masked her with an eclipse
If we were not already
divided by color we are now
luminously separate but equal
half of us clothed in shadows
down to the skin while
the other half wonders
Why is everything always
about not having power

For the Dead Whose Caskets Flowed Out of Graves
after the South Carolina Thousand-Year Flood (2015)

> *Roll, Jordan, roll*
> *Roll, Jordan, roll*
> *My soul arise in heaven, Lord*
> *for the year when Jordan roll*
>   —12 Years a Slave (2013)

One last parade   through haunted highways
Procession past   gators and moccasins
dead drifting   reincarnated
into a spectacle   by watery grave

Purgatory road to heaven   barricaded, delayed
A river runs through   the King's highway to glory
Lingering breaths   from a hurricane's shadow

Transparent souls laid   one on another
will screenplay   the Carolina docu-horror
weekend marathon of   films not shared from cutting room floors
This terror This blood   These screams Their drowning

These whips These chains   These night Their howling
No special effects   No stunt people needed
These bodies   can't wait for *Action!*
This is   the zombie   apocalypse they've been dying for

They can now look forward   to dying again for the world to see
after their last rites delivered   at the end of another thousand-year baptism
when God tempts His words   never again to destroy by water

Perhaps He just   cannot dam his tears
needs cheering up   by bodies seeding the earth's belly a second time

Mother Earth's   amniotic fluid rain

baptizing the unborn-undead   Lazarus reborn
waded with shrouded legs out   the tomb through lost souls
leaving behind these bodies   to travail in a hydraulic carriage

Bursting from this state's   insatiable womb
they are the lost dream of slave ships   wishing to breach Carolina shores
dreams stowed away in this vessel on   their backs looking up to midnight

suspending a crescent moon above   a lonely palmetto Manifest destiny
will not reach the auction block   All will not feel Jordan on their toes
Their voyage leads bodies   down the timeline past North Charleston

past Mother Emanuel   past an empty flagpole—wait...
Is Walter in there?   Is one of the Nine? Is it a desperate flag?
A-tisket A-tasket   We've lost our best-laid caskets

If one or all are soon   to breach another dam then
Roll, roll, roll on   to Jordan! Don't look back!
This is the year   for your souls to rise

Love Letter for South Carolina

You marched through me with torches
before I knew my hanged body was burning

whisked through my marrow before the bones were broken

I knew I had to fly from your prayers and good intentions
but the song of your scything accent nailed

my wings deep into your holy cross

This is the only way you know how to love
I test the limits of this relationship

to see if it is really how I wish to

launch myself into the afterlife
One minute I want you branded inside my cheeks

just to French kiss your sun

each time I open my crescent moon mouth
The next I feel you paintbrush my face with

Southern hospitality dipped in black bodies

a canvas slapped behind sharp-edged stars against
rusty bars waving crimson heritage over my bruised head

but I have nowhere else to go and no one to take me there

I've grown to expect your schizophrenia
which makes me a narcissist for thinking

I am better than you for remaining in your toxic space

I pretend not to see your gaping flaws and serve you
I smile at the palmetto trunk cracks in your lips

I tell my friends I'm in love when they cover their faces to

the scars you gave me even on our best days
If I were stronger I'd unleash my scorched tongue and

pray eagles that may come out as flightless birds

but the attempt gathers me
together for your next deafening slap

I'm yours for life

I wish your beatings were only BDSM
You seem more into necrophilia

reenacting death marches dressed in white instead of black

You romance me like your decrepit monuments
You bludgeon me to march over me again

Perhaps it's why you remain among

last in education and first in
domestic violence deaths

A Blind Man Gives You [In] Sight
after the 2017 Solar Eclipse

The backs of my eyelids are
reserved for celestial bodies
An upstart moon pauses between
two egos and a world goes dark
I call it Tuesday
when an upstart abysmal orange crater
passes through two congressional bodies
and the world loses sight
weeps and covers its eyes
stands still
I call it [insert] day
when a black body passes
through two or more egos
wearing blue
and goes blind
for light-years
Call me anything but blind
Who is anyone to call me
anything but a celestial body
The backs of my eyelids are
reserved for the heavens
I see holy lights tacked
bulleted through
sheets of blackness
My eyes are open
I see everything as it is
nothing as it should be
You see an eclipse and
open your eyes for
the first time

Plan B

for Big nose
It runs in the family
a mountain erupting
from fountains of family loins
Grandma gene-fed Daddy with it
and he spit it out onto my oily face
covered my whole body with it
B for *Big Bird beak*!
My feathers are a darker shade
B for Buzzard? Oh no!
Call me Black Falcon
Tears slide smooth down its slope
Rippling in pain as the nostrils flare
I am one Big snout
I root, I grunt, I snort
B for bullies who said
Hey! Tell us what it smells like in China with that thing!
Maybe I can dig there with it
pack a bag and swim through the earth
led by this golden shovel
past family loins that spawned it
B for blood bones, scars from whips
past singed psyches and too many games of the dozens
too many laughs at our own people
too many crabs in barrels
gawks at Big noses and Big lips
B for Big butts and thighs
B for Big brown eyes
B for Blistering tears running raw on jagged brown faces
Streaming from ravaged fountains
even hers
She walks out of the closed room slowly
head down
shuffling her tear-stained feet

Big brown eyes low
then straight at me
B for boy
He would've had your nose, she moans

Racism Is as American as _____

        _____ a race to be called

    World Champions

of an American sport

      _____ as biased as

        the American race

    The human race is un-American

Americans are as hyphenated as

    an Emily Dickinson poem

        broken into shards of color and class

    Now that's as American as

a sliced-up pie

    divided

        never symmetrical

    as hacked up as

bovine bodies in a butcher shop

      100% American prime cuts

        cooked rare but still bloody

      dripping as wet as dye on

a new flag

      Whether you stand or kneel before it

           the red drips into your eyes

      You become lost behind the bars of it

Now that's as American as

      prison bars

           where Americans divide into shards of color

      They know that being American

doesn't matter behind bars

      Stars don't twinkle there

           as on a spangled banner

      or in a patriotic song

as racist as

      calling someone else's native

           soil your Land of the Free

      as racist as

using their names

      for your ball teams

        hitting homeruns

    with their names on your chest

forgetting that you

    gave them those names

        Playing games with race

    Now that's just like

America's pastime

When a White Man in Camden Tells You to Act Like You Got Some Sense

                Daddy never called me outside to work on cars with him
I kneeled before Saturday morning cartoons
     while he prayed at the altar of a raised hood
            Peeking at him from inside the house
    the red glow of his Salem Lights
    in the car's dark temple seemed holy
              No mantle for automotive repair dropped from the sky
                  onto my shoulders when
                      he left in his chariot to the clouds

    I do not have his tools
    I do not know their names

    Fear weaves theatre with my puppet strings
    when I arrive at any repair shop
My tongue struggles violently to escape a bear trap of
inadequacy when asked about oils and fluids and gauges
         Waving a white flag to declare my fatherless condition
         concedes to moments of depression and paralysis

                    I am Zechariah
              father of John the Baptist
          tongue chained to the roof of my mouth
      not for lack of faith under the hooded temple
    but for the rabbit hole I hurtle through
        hoping to find Daddy in Wonderland with
            a scepter of manhood to anoint me
            gifts of mechanics, hunters, fishermen
                boils into my flesh

My fault   for staying asleep too long on Saturdays
    for waking up from Wonderland

    When a white man tries his best to conceal
his thirst for my blood outside his repair shop in Camden
on a cold Tuesday morning
                        barking instructions
like a plantation overseer on how to simply
move my broken down car from the
middle of the street to his parking lot six feet away

    Wonderland calls
and my bones answer
        with rigor mortis

my black pupils now pinballs crashing
      wildly into their white corners
He can't resist the grit of his teeth any longer

    Nigger, act like you got some sense

        I fall farther
                deeper
My head bangs against the rabbit hole
    My inner Alice cascades through its echoes

    I wish I could
Pray that this grave
leads me to Daddy
    to 1985
to the temple of free men
anywhere but your judgment
    your white privilege
        its handpicked
        fully equipped sons
            trained in the art of
                boyhood

Niger (or the Country with a Missing Letter)

Let's assume no one is to blame

The boy simply mispronounced an unfamiliar word
Only a few years removed from elementary school
he still lacked the cognitive development to remember
that a short vowel sound precedes a double consonant
and even in a gifted and talented pullout day session
his mind was too preoccupied with the peculiar
multicolored continental map to consider enunciation
to investigate the seemingly missing *G*
invisible like *G* is for god

He simply required an alternative pullout session with
the speech or reading specialist to fill in the chasm
between the cliff the boy should have leaped from in elementary
with eager toes and the cliff he appeared to be teetering
by his slick ball-bearing heels in middle-level language arts
backstroking his arms in the air to avoid the dark nebulous
valley of the missing letter like *G* is for gap

The teacher needed her rest away from four straight hours
entertaining the most promising minds of that
middle school class in a rural Carolina town
They had worn down her sharpness with intriguing
and tenacious question after question
She needed them to have the free time for her to recuperate
to gather her own ball bearings before collapsing
Had she heard the little white boy mispronounce the African country
she certainly would have corrected him (had she heard of it herself)
Why shouldn't she as a teacher of gifted students
although she accounted for no African studies in her curriculum

Even though half her class that day was black
she would not be expected by the principal, the district, the school board

not even her own conscience to help the students understand the culture
of an entire unknown continent with worlds of no significance
to Southern 1980s segregated rural life outside the school walls
If she did hear him say the wrong word
why would she be expected to correct him
She had to save her breath for the afternoon lessons
She had to replenish her energy instead of assisting him in finding
a missing letter like *G* is for Great Teacher Award

And what of the boy who opened the atlas
an obscure black boy drawn to world geography
while all the computers in the room were occupied
The others played Number Crunchers and Oregon Trail
Meanwhile, the boy awaited his turn by unearthing
undiscovered civilizations on globes and maps
No one told him he could not pursue Africa
After seven years of education, no one breathed into him
  that it was real
  that he could travel there
  that he had already been there in his blood
        his eyes
         the hue of his skin
No teacher warned him in classroom rules and procedures
that Africa was never to be spoken of
because the savages there still stalked the earth
thirsty for blood without reason
a race of vampires
right down to the babies he had seen in the commercials
starving for food and medical attention
It must have been a hoax to acquire more blood surreptitiously

But the glossy pages of the World Atlas tempted his fingers
The white boys in the class must have seen the glimmer
of magic in his eyes when they glanced over at him alone with the book
They had never desired his company or presence before
Something had awakened in him, and they had to know how

to cast it out and claim it as their own

This gun-shaped continent called out to him
with delicious tribal names bursting with knowledge and wisdom
He ran them across his tongue like the first lick of a Tootsie Roll pop
He dared not ask the teacher from her weary position
for their meanings or pronunciations
She may have been quick to bite down on him like the crunch of Mr. Owl

He simply glared into the Congo of the map while
the white boys gathered in silence
tongue whips extended
mouth firearms cocked and ready
and then the alert white scout pointed
Look, it's Nigger
and the celebratory laughter followed
dragging the missing letter from the
jungle like *G* is for *Got 'im!*

Had they all remained at the table to view
the landlocked country closer, they may have
perceived the other mighty territories it bordered
one of which is Chad
a name certainly borrowed by one of their ancestors
who taught their bloodlines to use the double *G*'s and short vowel *I*
The black boy had been quite familiar with the etymology
spewed from their mouths to acid his reclamation of self
the pride of cleansing their tonsils and
blasting hot ammunition through the heavy foreign
barbaric bushes with each trigger of the sensual *guh* sound

The fire in the boy's eyes precipitated into salty rain
dripping onto Africa that day, but it stopped
as abruptly as a sunny devil-beating-his-wife rain
The white boys may have snared him on the shores for the long
Middle Passage voyage, yet he would escape

if those boys captured the missing *G*
Then the black boy would from that day until now
aim with precision the sharp-speared *juh* of the country's name and

reclaim the long *I* within

You've Heard This Before

daddy dies

boy leaves
boy touches everything with his feelings
boy stumbles through teenage years
boy mines girls for his daddy's love lost
boy terrorizes his mama because he can
boy despises the name Jr.
      changes his whole name

boy has sons with the first girl he lays with
      thinks it's love
boy embraces sons
      too hard
boy leaves girl
      tortured her enough
boy's sons rebel
boy named no son Jr. nor imprisoned them
      behind the bars of III

boy becomes man
man teaches other boys
      longs for his sons
new boys with daddy gaps stretch out on him in droves
man searches for his daddy and sons in the crowd
man crouches in the slot between the *J* and *R* to weep

new boys stray from man
man can't play father or son to anyone
man faintly hears daddy calling for Jr. again

Snap Beans

Scrooge McDuck fingers
swim through green gems
in a Tupperware pool

Young, mannish hands
crave a decadence
they don't understand

Husky, plump stems release
their essence into my bowl
and I play with delight

find them, lose them
and find them again
in my palms

Riches don't just buy
freedom in this bowl
Emerald waves gather here

ebbing and flowing like
garden-grown waterfalls
much more fulfilling than

aching my thumbs
unzipping the stems
rescuing the beans

My fingers forget they're tired
Mama says, *Shuck dem beans
wit your thumbs, boy*

Unknown somebodies ached their fingers
their backs, their glistening brows

to secure the stimulus for my elation

Stalks in my bowl
must be relieved
by my thuggish hands

The Black Body Is a Wind Chime

Perfect for whistling bullets through
Singing discordant yet delicious screams
Symphonic scent of burning flesh
Climbing Kilimanjaro leaving trails of blood
The black body is a piccolo
Blown into but never kissed
Blistering white lips race to apply breath to it
But never desire real intimacy
Muscular music makes men mad
With black notes filling their nostrils
String the black bare skin bamboo together
And call them bones of holy ghosts
Sold on the auction block to the highest sinner
A chanting wind whips resistance through them

I'm Human Too

He said this on our business trip the same night
he told me he made money pimping on the side

Something about the glasses at the end of his nose
the gray, wiry strands of hair struggling to escape his rambling

the limping leg like Atlas anchoring the world of his potbelly
and the gapped teeth occasionally releasing the crotchety tongue

framed my disbelief. I thought, Why didn't he just burst in
to stop us dead in our tracks on the motel bathroom floor

where my knees were giving out, dug into the diseased
linoleum until I stood to seed her enduring mouth

rewarding the patient tongue, a legacy
for daughters she may never have

I lost focus before the great eruption
stowing away in the memory of scars

on her ripe bottom from an apparent
bout with chicken pox as a child

before the wig and makeup from
her pimp, my roommate, groomed her

Who is more human: the man who
spews out a lamb to the slaughter

or the man who weeps
as he devours its bleating

Yeah, I guess the old man had the right to say it

with us negotiating the finish a wall away

but so did she. I may have erupted in tears if that
became the fruit of her lips instead of her asking

Are you a cop

We're Talking about Practice

selected words from an excerpt of the infamous Allen Iverson interview arranged according to frequency

Sixer deteriorate downhill contradicting press conference ball league 48 minutes winner city trading coaching staff yadayada die funny critique criticized criticizing automatically strange honored microphone matters obviously cool tough corner daughter daughters daughters trade trade players players ain't ain't upset upset praise praise your your love love hear hear hell hell tired tired you're you're practicing practicing plays plays superstar superstar cry cry problem problem court court organization organization everything everything hurts hurts hurts deal deal deal job job job paid paid paid better better better best best best Philadelphia Philadelphia Philadelphia basketball basketball basketball world world world problems problems problems simple simple simple team team team everybody everybody everybody people people people people Allen Allen Allen Allen Iverson Iverson Iverson Iverson man man man man human human human human play play play play talk talk talk talk Larry Larry Larry Larry y'all y'all y'all y'all y'all shit shit shit shit shit Coach Coach Coach Coach Coach MVP MVP MVP MVP MVP lost lost lost lost lost lose lose lose lose lose lose teammates teammates teammates teammates teammates teammates teammates we we we we we we we mean mean mean mean mean mean mean mean franchise franchise franchise franchise franchise franchise franchise franchise franchise that's that's that's that's that's that's that's that's that's that's Brown Brown Brown Brown Brown Brown Brown Brown Brown Brown player player player player player player player player player player player a a a a a a a a a a a game game game game game game game game game game game hurt hurt hurt hurt hurt hurt hurt hurt hurt hurt hurt hurt hurt we're we're we're we're we're we're we're we're we're we're we're we're we're we're we're we're we're not not not not not not not not not not not not not not not not not not talking talking talking talking talking talking talking talking talking talking talking talking talking talking talking talking talking talking my my my my my my my my my my my my my my my my my my practice that that that that that that that that that that that that that that that that that that that that that that that that I'm I'm I'm I'm I'm I'm I'm I'm I'm I'm I'm I'm I'm I'm I'm I'm I'm I'm I'm I'm I'm I'm I'm I'm I'm I'm I'm me me me me me me me me me me me me me me me me me me me me me me me me me me me me me me me about you you you you you you you you you you you you you you you you you you you you you you you you you you you you you you you you you you you you you you you you I I I I I I I I I I I I I I I I I I I I I I I I I I I I I I I I I I I I I I I I I I I I I I I I I I I I I I I I I I I I I I I I I I I I

His Majesty

Purple Rain in the VCR
Fast forward to the Scene
He massages between her thighs
His fingers disappear and reappear
The camera blacks out the spot
our eyes glued to it
glancing half seconds at her head
tilted upward to his heaven

Rewind back to her act of sacrifice
Ready to be his disciple at the lake
she is an angel
she is a mermaid
yet he is even more unattainable

Stop the tape
We go to my bedroom
We role play
We are Prince and Darling Nikki
My fingers search her darkness
We plunge headlong into Lake Minnetonka
We both become his disciples
We worship on our knees
to the sound of purple

I Pass Liberty Seafood Every Day

I skirt the procession of fish lovers as
they park on the other side of the street
and control oncoming traffic with no more
than their wish-a-nigga-would eyes
into the cave of painted cinder blocks for

raw fragments of a night's dinner
But I do not go inside
It would be disrespectful
This is now hallowed ground to me
I cannot go where by a miracle of words

she fed thousands with tales of fish
I have lived in Sumter for eight years
I know every shortcut and back road
I have taken my children to Swan Lake
Who can forget the time they threw up

from eating too much pizza
and getting on the jungle gym
I lived in the apartment complex
with the dead body found
in the parking lot where I witnessed

brothers giving dap with concealed
powder packs between their fingers
I have toured churches searching for the
same god who set me on this pilgrimage
I met her nanny who told me stories

of her now famous prodigy li'l Lynn Finney
But I am no closer to Lynn than every time
I see her after her readings and
the words are snatched from my throat or

they become so utterly mortifying

I wish I were a fish ready to kneel before
the fishmonger priest who chants
Head off and split with a swipe of his cleaver so I
dare not enter the holy Liberty Seafood fish market
because I feel gutless enough already

The Body Is a Door

> *Every door is a lesson in leaving*
> —Susan Laughter Meyers

      The last two letters of the word *door*
indicate an alternative
      The first two letters denote an action

Yoda told us like this
         Do—or do not. There is no try
     commanding doors like the master he was
saying, *Door, do not.*
        Don't try me.

We walk through the word *door*
     when we become souls
buildings of flesh and bone we open
     our eyes in every morning

        If the eyes are the windows to the soul
     then why hasn't anyone shown us
how to open the door

It really pisses us off in the afterlife
     when we discover
there are no doors
     only dimensions
        The o's in *door* are simply portals
           windows of déjà vu
        where we see in a mirror darkly
          what we can master on the other side

This body is a dimension
     a lesson before death

a firmament to be commanded

without a key

Skinny Boy

Weave a house salad into my pores
long enough for me to marinate in green

Fat shame was a soggy wet dream when
Rail thin was my answer to *What you gonna be*

when you grow up? First impressions
cut like a diamond fist

slicing away 99% body fat from my psyche
leaving stains of insecurity in the hallway mirror

of our trailer. I dreamed for a funhouse mirror to be
my shadow / my belly / tattoos of stretch marks

Lap band surgery would be the last resort for Star Jones
if we could have exchanged bellies. That is until

metabolism lost its libido in my waist and
left a suicide note with blood drippings in the art form of

tattooed stretch marks. Crop circles taste better harvested
from my seasoned skin. Nobody cares about a normal-sized boy

in the South. You either have to be too fat,
too skinny, too sick, too black, too light-skinned, too

smart, too dumb, or too tired of it all to stay
Nobody wants you to be average

The mirror into mediocre doesn't work that way
Let my uncle tell it: *A potbelly looks good on you*

Let baby love tell it: *Boy, you can still get it*

Tell that to the 12-year-old boy I buried

under pillows wishing at night that I could
devour them and shame the devil for birthing me

into the height and width of a cross

Down South

Five-and-dime. Antique store. Cash and
carry. Drugstore. Barbershop. Shoe shop.
Record store. Bridal boutique. Dive bar.

You're on your knees digging through
the catacombs of small business
all hemorrhaging green

The law of the South says
you can't get blood from a turnip
You wish you could flip down

transparencies of time to see
the old shops in their heyday
when dusty dirt roads

exhaled clouds of anticipation
and alleys in the crevices of town
felt no pressure to be firm asphalt

Up north the empty buildings
are called *abandoned*
Down here they look neglected

like the little girl
pretending to be princess
of her trailer park

parading with her wand
dancing in her tutu
before her uncle's rape

My old barber was also a butcher by day
He could chuck away at me like a lumberjack

or finesse me like a surgeon

but no one mourned cattle
outside his shop
or lost knuckleheads

like up north

I Was Born with No Middle Name

my first and last amputated at the waist
so the more desirable parts of me can live

but people still look at my deformity and ask

Where is the rest of you

I asked Grandma why she
never gave Daddy one either

She said nothing

speaking its absence
and mine
into existence

birthing a dream
she would not remember
from her weary nostrils

declaring in her brilliance
Who needs a crown
he will never wear

The Body Is a God

When it is born we kiss it with
prayers trembling from our lips
We swaddle our tongues in silence
to anoint the swaddled flesh in our arms

When it dies we kneel before its altar
prepared for the ground and beg with tears
for our hearts not to escape our chests
We cycle the altar with the rhythm

of a parted sea in awe of the
suspended waters on either side
We fear one day not being able
to penetrate our own casket thrones

We worship every scar and cover it
We exalt every curve and twerk it
We extol every orifice and fill it
This body is a church

with steeple pointing to its death
and buried knees on an altar
in the temple of our bellies
If we worship enough gods

we pray they will reciprocate
We neglect our own holiness
chasing a YHWH in others
This body is such a supreme deity

that the very god we have
never seen birthed itself
a body only to be crushed
by the very gods it created

The Nightclub // Is a Funeral // Is a Nightclub

We're already dressed
    to the nines
heavy hanging loops
    calculated tears
Shadows already color
    our garments in grief
and the slow drag
    of our bottomless cups
tempts our drops to refill them
    with nectar dripping
from black roses

    Primal screams
in the fetal position
    on dance floors
One two-step
    then grinding
our teeth on caskets
    to wake the dead
in both buildings
    Didn't you see your
church members at both
    Didn't you see your
pastor offer your tithes
    with club stamp
on his hands to God
    with that booming
bass rumbling
    between his eyes
or was it
    the telltale heart
of the deceased
    He did not save them
the last dance

      at last call
their souls refusing
      death but not heaven
with velvet rope
      blocked by lucifer
coated with the finest
      sapphires and emeralds
at the door
      He is the only one
capable of giving
      an accurate eulogy
for everyone inside

      I'm leaving
before somebody
      shoots up the place with
gang war glock or
      racist .45 to raise
the [Dylan] roof and
      a [Omar Ma] teen
like a mother never could

      Either way
the angels will be last to
      remove the blood and bodies
and turn out the lights
      before the screams of
blood and sweat and tears
      peal through the walls
with no windows

How Not to Dissect a Frog

Put it in water
closed in a Ziploc bag
Place the bag in a freezer overnight
When it still has a heartbeat by morning
question nature
question the nature within you
question your thirst for
the sight of animal entrails
question why you must show this to
your science teacher
question the science of dissecting
and why it is not rather an art
question why you did not just
use alcohol on a cotton swab
like any other biologist
Leave the block of ice in the sunlight
on the kitchen windowsill
Question your removal
of the cold-blooded frog
suspended in ice from the bag
Answer with you are not a scientist
Answer you are an artist

In Which People Say *You Look Like Buuud from The Cosby Show*

          First of all
I wouldn't be taking random
misogynistic advice on girls from
my mythical brother whom no one
has even seen on camera

          I mean
was dude in jail?
Did he sell drugs?
Did he have multiple baby mamas
      ... or some other black stereotype?

          I mean
I thought this show was
supposed to be progressive

          I mean
did dude drug and rape
countless women
which got him cut from
the very first season?

I've had my share of friends who were girls
None of them changed my name
      and in that way
wasn't Rudy ahead of her time?
Isn't she the ultimate feminist?
Not taking patriarchy from boys
          [not even from her own father]

      ... and why weren't my parents ever seen on the show?
Did they abandon me?
Wouldn't they too have a brownstone in Brooklyn
      ... or did I just take the bus or train from Harlem

                    [with my dream-deferred self]
or another borough every time I wanted to
argue with Rudy about my own name?
Why couldn't Rudy learn any life lessons from my folks
        ... or do the Huxtables have the monopoly on
        educating America on uppity blackness?

        ... and after all of those years
at the pinnacle American house of negritude
why wouldn't we ever talk about being black?
                        [see Tiger Woods]
Why didn't Claire Huxtable as an attorney ever warn us
about police brutality? about keeping our mouths shut
if detained? about them not caring if our parents were
doctors, lawyers, judges, politicians, or even
police men and women themselves

                I mean
they didn't live on Sesame Street
so I know there was crime around

                I mean
I probably should have hung out with
Fat Albert and the gang if I wanted
to know what life would really be like
        ... and still wouldn't even
one of that gang have died from some
American tragedy?

        ... and wouldn't Dr. Heathcliff Huxtable himself
have warned me about making babies before I was ready
seeing as I didn't have any real parents on the show?

                I mean
he was an ob-gyn
Wouldn't he have thought a black boy should have

that talk, let alone with his own son?

                I mean
with four daughters
wouldn't he of all people have understood
telling a young black kid in New York
about birth control
      … and wouldn't that be a zerbert to my cheek
if he gave me condoms like he gave
Cousin Pam birth control?

I might have been better off staying at home
with my imaginary family for my
imaginary brother to at least attempt to school me
on reality instead of my being
so disillusioned by the Huxtable fantasy
that I would not even be worthy of
the name my mama gave me

            … I mean
if she really did give me a name anyway

      … or
maybe Rudy was just softening the blow
Maybe I was an orphan
and they just didn't want to tell me
Maybe I was found in a dumpster
like in Tupac's "Brenda's Got a Baby"
and given a chance by a black man on a TV show
Maybe he saved me from being killed on the street by police
Maybe I kept coming back to the Huxtable house
not to be a statistic
      … isn't that the kind of love we crave?
overseen by TV camera angels
and boom mic archangels
and the heavenly showbiz lights above us

and the glory of the laugh track engulfing us in prayer
creating a fake family in a studio
because the pain of acknowledging
reality is too great?
Isn't that what Bill Cosby did?

    Didn't we all wish we were Huxtable?
Wasn't Bud just another one
of his illegitimate children?
        Aren't I ...?
                ... I mean
                            first of all

      aren't we all ...?

Going to Court in My Hometown

It is morning　　　　　　and no one here　　　　　takes my face seriously
We are relics　　　　　　　　one to another
I'm not sure　　　　　　if this place is　　　Old or New Testament
or if it is I　　　　who is old　　　　　or new
I smell embers　　　from something　　　not burning on the outside
　　　　　but I know　　　　hell is near
　　　underneath my tongue　　every time my lips part
　　　　　　　　to curse this ground
　　　　　I see flames in their flesh　　　wailing in their eyes
They are the rich man　　　　　　　　　　who beseeches Lazarus
　　　　to place a drop　　　of water　　on his tongue
　　　　　　　　in his fiery afterlife
　　　　　　I can　only drop　　one tear
I recall　　　driving drunk here one night　　coming to a stop sign
　　　　　with hallucinations　　　　　　of running it
to jump my car　　over train tracks ahead　　on a hill
　　　　Had I gotten　　　　　　　　stuck in the stars
　　　　my dead body　　　　　　　would be　　god
Today my limp body　　　　is next to my name
　　　　　in a ledger　　　　　marked paid
I am the corpse　　　　of the kid　　　　who got hit
　　　by a train in　　　　　　*Stand By Me*
At least　　　　　I still get　　　　to look up
　　　at the stars　　　flat on my back
Buzzards will　　　　　eventually circle
by morning
They look　　　　away from me
as I leave town
　　　　I have followed them　　　　as far as　　　　I can go

The Body Is a Rustic Bag

A vagabond drapes it over his shoulder
It whistles with each tumbling step
and sags heavier as his grip loosens
It chimes with the humble gifts inside
He stops along the road for rest

The bag takes a new shape in the dust
He reaches in and pulls out a map
marked with every place he's been
He won't get to every other spot
The dust will reclaim his sack of bones

Not Stopping at a Police Checkpoint at 5 AM after Buffing Floors All Night and Feeling High from the Fumes

I am Crispus Attucks-ing my way
through the first stage of *Inception*

A ride under the tongue of dawn through the gullet
of the South is the face of the deep before *Let there be*

My buckshot eyes are staring down the
snake hole barrel of an officer's peacemaker

I may prefer the bullet to the venom

Trunk of a black Oldsmobile Cutlass Supreme
rattles by to the beat of *Stankonia*

I have half a heart to yell in protest
wearing sackcloth, heaping ashes on my head

Big and Dre ain't never doing another album!
The car stalls at the traffic light I didn't reach

then restarts after two attempts at the ignition
Adorable the way a car tells you its name when it starts

The other heart half violently attempts a jailbreak
from its straightjacket between the deputies' eyes

Every heart attack is a microaggression
The body prays for freedom but we oppress her

with life

A glance at the horizon before the badges
wreck me to the pavement wondering

if Zion will remember her daddy this morning
You give your daughter an African name

so you can hold the distant Motherland close
like you can't hold the little girl now

The glory of god rests on Mount Zion
where angels ascend and descend

lifting me from the street and speaking truths
in unknown tongues to me but apparently known

to the sheriff's finest because when I touch down
I am doing 70 on the long highway home

white feathers pirouetting above the
dash to the beats of *So Fresh, So Clean*

with nobody dope as me

Acknowledgments

"America." was published in *Hand in Hand: Poets Respond to Race*.

"black body be like" and "We're Talking about Practice" were published in *The James Franco Review*.

"Battle Royal" was published in *Pennsylvania English*.

"For the Dead" and "the body is a cave" were published in *Connotation Press*.

"A Blind Man Gives You [In] Sight" was published in *SYZYGY: The Poetry Invitational*.

"Plan B" was published in *The Baltimore Review*.

"When a White Man in Camden" and "Niger" were published in *Drunk in a Midnight Choir*.

"You've Heard This Before" was published by *The Good Men Project*.

"I'm Human Too" was published in *HEArt Online Journal*.

"Skinny Boy" was published in *Pittsburgh Poetry Review*.

"Down South" was published in *Charleston Currents*.

"Hymn to the Tiki God" was published in *South Florida Poetry Journal*.

"Snap Beans" has been accepted for publication by *African American Review*.

"The Black Body Is a Wind Chime" was published in *Thrush Poetry Journal*.

Thank You(s)

The whims of a country boy from Bamberg, South Carolina, have amounted to this. Before being declared a poet, I was a young nature explorer, a believer, a lover and romantic, husband, ex-husband, father, and in some respects, a dreamer, yet all the while I wrote. I wrote to bear out a gift I neither understood nor embraced. However, with this collection, I embrace these labels that I float through from time to time and understand them much more.

To my enduring inner circle: my mother Ozella, stepfather Donald, sister Yojuana, and grandmother Roseanne, I am nothing if not a dreamer, and you four are always there to catch me when I awake.

To my beloved editors Roberto and Lynne, I relish in the opportunity to have you polish my words so that they shine. I love the philosophy of Get Fresh. I pray many years for the revolution.

To Cortney and Sharan, your words about my work break me down to my core. I kneel before greater wordsmiths.

To all my fellow writing and artist fellows whom I've met at The Watering Hole, Callaloo, Vermont Studio Center, Weymouth Center for the Arts, and Virginia Center for the Creative Arts, you've made me believe the word *poet* could be assigned to my humble existence.

To my gladiator mentors: Mariahadessa Ekere Tallie, the blazing sun that you are warms me. You always hold the mirror in front of me and dare me to stare back. To Jane Shore, the door of your heart invigorates me with the excitement of a gold rush. Thank you for allowing me to sit at your feet and for performing surgery on my words. To Greg Pardlo, I will always strive to—as you told me— "let the Hulk come out on the page". To Marjory Wentworth, you believe in me so hard I can't think of myself in any other way—bless.

To my co-founder and co-conspirator Al Black, I will always be there to play Robin to your Batman. Our work with Poets Respond to Race will stand but only in the shadow of our friendship.

To my many colleagues in education over the years, quoting the Georgia Mass Choir, *Nooooo, I'm not tired yet*. I'm glad we were able to share war stories to keep each other sane. I'm always here for you.

To my editor-in-chief April Michelle Bratten, you've given me the chance to learn this business beyond the page. You are a gatekeeper to so many poets' dreams. Thank you for letting me tag along for the ride.

To my future dissertation advisor Michael T. Williamson, you're the best for believing in me and letting me share my work in your space. I pray we get this thing done right.

Many thanks to all journals who have published my words in your hallowed spaces.

Finally, to anyone inspired by my words past, present, and future, this is for you. We are in this craft together. We are in this conversation together. We are in this life together. I am yours for the taking.

About the Author

Len Lawson received a B.S. in Business Administration from Winthrop University, an M.A. in English from National University, and is currently pursuing a Ph.D. in English Literature & Criticism at Indiana University of Pennsylvania. He was the Morris College 2011-12 Advisor of the Year and 2012-13 Professor of the Year, along with being a 2013 Excellence in Teaching Award winner from South Carolina Independent Colleges & Universities (SCICU). His scholarly article "Back to the Future: Approaches to Best Practices in Reflective Teaching" appeared in *Cultivating Visionary Leadership by Learning for Global Success: Beyond the Language and Literature Classroom* (Cambridge Scholars Publishing, 2015). Len is the author of the chapbook *Before the Night Wakes You* (Finishing Line Press, 2017) and co-editor of *Hand in Hand: Poets Respond to Race* (Muddy Ford Press, 2017).

Len won the 2016 *Jasper Magazine* Artist of the Year Award in Literary Arts and was named among "Ten South Carolina Poets to Watch" by the Richland County Library in 2018. He was also named a 2018 Sumter, SC Top 20 Professionals under 40 nominee. Len has been a multiple-time Pushcart Prize and *Best of the Net* nominee as well. He earned a fellowship to the Callaloo Creative Writing Workshop in Barbados facilitated by 2015 Pulitzer Prize-winning poet Greg Pardlo. He has also earned fellowships from Vermont Studio Center, Virginia Center for the Creative Arts, and became the inaugural winner of the 2018 Susan Laughter Meyers Poetry Fellowship at the Weymouth Center for the Arts sponsored by the North Carolina Poetry Society. Len has been a finalist for the 2015 inaugural Berfrois Poetry Prize, the 2016 Mississippi Review Poetry Prize, the 2016 Yellow Chair Review Chapbook Competition, and the 2018 Gigantic Sequins Poetry Prize. His poetry has also been featured in coffee shops and transit buses in the Columbia, SC metro area.

His poetry appears in several anthologies and journals including *Callaloo Journal*, *African American Review*, *Verse Daily*, and *Charleston Currents*, selected by South Carolina Poet Laureate Marjory Wentworth.

www.ingramcontent.com/pod-product-compliance
Lightning Source LLC
Chambersburg PA
CBHW060501010526
44118CB00018B/2497